Marii

Book

Juicy Marinade Recipes for Chicken, Beef, Pork, And More!

BY: Valeria Ray

License Notes

Copyright © 2019 Valeria Ray All Rights Reserved

All rights to the content of this book are reserved by the Author without exception unless permission is given stating otherwise.

The Author have no claims as to the authenticity of the content and the Reader bears all responsibility and risk when following the content. The Author is not liable for any reparations, damages, accidents, injuries or other incidents occurring from the Reader following all or part of this publication.

Table of Contents

Introduction 6

1. Liliko'I Marinade 7

2. Spicy Pomegranate Marinade 9

3. Marinade II 11

4. Easy Middle Eastern Marinade 13

5. Delicious Beef Marinade 15

6. Lemon Spice Marinade 17

7. Vinaigrette Marinade 19

8. Creamy Spiced Marinade for Chicken 21

9. Creamy Mint Chicken Marinade Murgh Masala 23

10. Asian Prawns Marinade 25

11. Creamy Yogurt Marinade 27

12. Pineapple Marinade for Chicken 29

13. Rosemary and Garlic Marinade 31

14. Orange Juice and Honey Marinade for Chicken BBQ ... 33

15. Papaya and Onion Steak Marinade 35

16. Brown Sugar and Vinegar Marinade for Steak 37

17. Balsamic Rosemary Marinade 39

18. Brown Sugar and Maple Syrup Marinade 41

19. Mustard and Vinegar Marinade 43

20. Spicy Fish Marinade 45

21. Dijon Mustard and White Vinegar Fish Marinade 47

22. Spicy Yogurt Beef Marinade 49

23. Hot Apple Cider Beef Marinade 51

24. Brandy Marinade 53

25. Bourbon Marinade 55

26. Pepper Sage Marinade 57

27. Cranberry Marinade 59

28. Honey Garlic Pork Marinade 61

29. Garlic Basil Marinade 63

30. Citrus Marinade 65

Conclusion 67

About the Author 68

Author's Afterthoughts 70

Introduction

Marinades are a centuries old technique to infuse flavor into any dish. Sweet and spicy, or thick and creamy, marinades are super easy to bring together and help elevate your meal to another level!

So, go ahead, bring alive the flavors of these delicious marinade recipes: earthy, rich, aromatic, softly sweet, hot and sour. Infused with fresh, leafy herbs and fragrant spices, your marinade options are now endless!

1. Liliko'I Marinade

Sweet, tart, and fragrant, this Hawaiian marinade is perfect for delicate protein such as seafood.

Total Time: 1h 30m

Servings: Makes ½ cup

Ingredients:

- ¼ cup liliko'i (passion fruit) pulp (see this page)
- 2 tablespoons rice vinegar
- 2 teaspoons Dijon mustard
- 1 tablespoon sugar
- ¼ cup neutral oil or olive oil
- ¼ teaspoon kosher salt
- ¼ teaspoon freshly ground black pepper

Directions

In a blender, combine the liliko'i pulp with the rice vinegar, mustard, sugar, oil, salt, and pepper and process on high speed for 2 to 3 minutes, until smooth. Use right away or transfer to an airtight jar or bottle and store in the refrigerator for up to 1 week.

2. Spicy Pomegranate Marinade

Looking for a delicious marinade for your dinner protein? Try out this delicious pomegranate marinade!

Total Time: 20 mins

Servings per recipe: 1

Ingredients

- 1 tsp chili powder
- 2 tbsp. dark soy sauce
- 2 tsp ground cumin
- 2 tbsp. olive oil
- 1/2 lemon, juiced
- 3 tbsp. pomegranate molasses

Directions

Combine together all the ingredients.

Add in desired meat and coat with marinade generously.

Refrigerator overnight before cooking.

3. Marinade II

Here's a delicious Mongolian marinade recipe for a quick dinner option!

Prep Time: 5 mins

Total Time: 10 mins

Servings per recipe: 4

Ingredients

- 1 tsp olive oil
- 1/2 tsp ginger powder
- 1 tbsp. minced garlic
- 1/2 C. soy sauce
- 1/2 C. water
- 1/4 C. brown sugar

Directions

In a wok, heat oil and sauté the ginger and garlic till aromatic.

Add the water, soy sauce and sugar and cook till sugar dissolves, stirring continuously.

Boil, then reduce the heat to low.

Simmer till the desired thickness of the sauce.

4. Easy Middle Eastern Marinade

This recipe works as a base for any Middle Easter inspired meat or veggie dish.

Total Time: 30 minutes

Servings: 1 ½ cups

Ingredients:

- ½ cup olive oil
- ½ cup onion, diced
- 2 lemons, juiced
- 5 tbsp garlic, minced
- 1 tbsp cilantro, chopped
- 1 tbsp cumin
- tsp bay leaves
- 2 tsp paprika
- ½ tsp turmeric

Directions:

Add all of the ingredients to an airtight container, shake and store in your fridge.

When ready to use, marinate your ingredients in a separate container for up to 6 hours in fridge. Follow the recipe for whatever dish you are preparing.

5. Delicious Beef Marinade

This marinate is perfect for any Middle Eastern inspired meat or veggie dish.

Total Time: 25 minutes

Servings: 3 ½ cups

Ingredients:

- 1 onion, chopped finely
- ½ cup lemon juice
- ½ cup olive oil
- ½ cup ginger, fresh
- 1 tbsp parsley, minced
- 2 tbsp soy sauce
- 1 tbsp cumin, ground
- 1 tbsp chili powder
- 2 tsp sherry
- 1 tbsp garlic, minced
- 1 tsp oregano
- 1 tsp turmeric
- 1 tsp black pepper, cracked

Directions:

Combine the ingredients in a container with a lid and store in fridge.

When ready to use, marinate your beef in a separate container for up to 4 to 6 hours, then cook according to the individual recipe.

6. Lemon Spice Marinade

Want to glam up a meal? This lemony marinade is perfectly balanced in terms of flavor!

Total Time: 10 minutes

Servings: 2

Ingredients:

- ¼ cup lemon juice
- 2 tbsp plain yogurt
- 1 ½ tsp honey
- ¼ tsp cumin
- ¼ tsp cinnamon
- ¼ tsp ginger
- ¼ cup EVOO
- ¼ tsp salt and pepper

Directions:

Start by whisking the Ingredients together and season with salt and pepper to taste. You want the marinade to be soft and smooth.

Refrigerate until ready to use, store excess marinade in fridge.

7. Vinaigrette Marinade

This vinaigrette can be served with meat dishes or tossed with a salad and used as a marinade!

Total Time: 10 to 12 minutes

Servings: 2

Ingredients:

- 2/3 cup olive oil
- 2 tbsp lemon juice
- 1 tbsp vinegar, apple cider
- 1 1/2 tsp paprika
- 1 tsp cumin
- 1 tbsp garlic, minced
- 1 pinch pepper, cayenne
- 4 tsp parsley, dried
- 1 tsp salt and pepper

Directions:

Add all of the Ingredients into a container with a lid that can be put in the fridge. Shake or whisk together.

Taste the marinade to make sure it meets your satisfaction. Adjust seasonings, if needed.

8. Creamy Spiced Marinade for Chicken

The addition of thick cream to the marinade makes this a delicious tenderizer for tougher meats.

Total Time: 1h 45m

Serves: 6

Ingredients:

- 1 lb. yogurt
- 2 tbsp. thick cream
- 1 tbsp. ginger paste
- 1 tbsp. garlic paste
- 1 tbsp. lemon juice
- Salt to taste
- 1 tbsp. cumin powder
- 6-8 green chilies, chopped finely
- 3 tbsp. cilantro leaves
- 2 tbsp. almond paste (optional)

Directions:

Mix together all ingredients.

Use or store for up to 1 week, refrigerated

9. Creamy Mint Chicken Marinade Murgh Masala

This delicious recipe gets its green hue from the fresh mint and cilantro leaves added in!

Total Time: 2h

Serves: 8

Ingredients:

- 2 1-inch piece ginger, roughly chopped
- 8-10 cloves garlic, roughly chopped
- ½ cup fresh cilantro leaves, chopped
- 4 tbsp. fresh mint leaves, chopped
- 6 green chilies
- ½ cup yogurt
- Salt to taste

Instructions:

Combine the green chilies, ginger, garlic, cilantro, and mint leaves and grind together.

Combine this mixture with yogurt and add salt to taste.

This marinade should be used for up to 1 hour when marinating chicken.

Use right away and store for 1 week in a fridge.

10. Asian Prawns Marinade

This recipe makes for a delicious and crunchy prawns marinade that can be used in stir frys!

Total Time: 30m

Servings: 6

Ingredients:

- 40 large prawns
- 2 tsp soy sauce
- Salt to taste
- Pepper to taste
- 8 tbsp. corn starch
- 2 tsp red chili sauce

Instructions:

1. Mix together all marinate ingredients and allow prawns to marinate for at least 20 minutes before deep frying!

2. Enjoy!

11. Creamy Yogurt Marinade

This mildly spiced yogurt marinade is guaranteed to be a regular for family nights!

Total Time: 45m

Servings: 6

Ingredients:

Marinade -

- 2 lb. chicken, cut into 8-10 pieces
- 1 tbsp garlic
- ½ tbsp ginger
- 1 cup yogurt
- 4 onions, sliced
- 4 green chilies, sliced
- 1 tsp cumin
- 1 whole garam masala powder
- 2 tbsp. almond paste
- Salt

Directions:

Combine all ingredients together and allow chicken to marinate for at least 2 hours and up to 8! Grill or bake according to preference.

12. Pineapple Marinade for Chicken

This is a sweet and fruity marinade recipe - very simple and full of flavor!

Yields: 2 cups

Time: 10 mins.

Ingredients:

- 1 cup pineapple (crushed)
- ½ cup ketchup
- 4 tablespoons vinegar
- 4 garlic cloves (minced)
- 1 teaspoon ginger powder
- 2 tablespoons soya sauce
- ½ teaspoon salt

Directions:

Add to food processor, pineapple, soy sauce, vinegar, ginger powder, olive oil and salt. Blend well.

Now add garlic cloves and ketchup, stir until combine.

13. Rosemary and Garlic Marinade

Rosemary and garlic, a great combination and it enhances the flavor of the chicken.

Yields: ¾ cups

Time: 10 mins.

Ingredients:

- 2 tablespoons dried rosemary
- 4 garlic cloves (minced)
- 1 teaspoon chili flakes
- 4 tablespoons lemon juice
- 1 teaspoon mustard paste
- 1-inch ginger slice (minced)
- 3 tablespoons vinegar
- ½ teaspoon salt
- ½ teaspoon black pepper

Directions:

Combine in a large bowl, minced garlic, dried rosemary, lemon juice, chili flakes, minced ginger, olive oil, vinegar, pepper and salt. Combine and mix well.

14. Orange Juice and Honey Marinade for Chicken BBQ

This is a perfect marinade for your BBQ Chicken. Sticky honey combined with freshly squeezed orange juice gives the chicken a beautiful color and a great flavor.

Yields: 1 ½ cups

Time: 8 mins.

Ingredients:

- 1 cup orange juice
- 4 tablespoons honey
- 1-inch ginger slice (chopped)
- 1 teaspoon thyme
- 4-5 garlic cloves (chopped)
- 1 teaspoon chili flakes
- 1 teaspoon dry coriander powder
- 2 tablespoons soya sauce
- 1 teaspoon salt
- ¼ teaspoon black pepper

Directions:

Take a large size bowl, add honey, orange juice, soya sauce, chopped garlic, thyme, chili flakes, chopped ginger, salt, coriander powder and black pepper. Mix thoroughly.

15. Papaya and Onion Steak Marinade

With this marinade you will enjoy the flavor of tropical fruit and a tinge of heat to your steak.

Yields: 2 cups

Time: 10 mins.

Ingredients:

- 3 tablespoons dried rosemary
- 1 cup papaya puree
- 1 teaspoon onion powder
- 4 garlic cloves (minced)
- 2 tablespoons lemon juice
- 1-inch ginger slice (minced)
- 3 tablespoons vinegar
- 3 tablespoons olive oil
- ½ teaspoon salt
- 1 teaspoon black pepper

Directions:

In a blender add olive oil, papaya puree, vinegar, onion powder, lemon juice, minced ginger, salt, garlic, rosemary and black pepper. Blend well.

16. Brown Sugar and Vinegar Marinade for Steak

This Brown Sugar and Vinegar Marinade paints every bite with flavor.

Yields: 1 ¾ cups

Time: 8 mins.

Ingredients:

- 3 tablespoons brown sugar
- 1 tablespoon garlic powder
- 1 teaspoon chili flakes
- 2 tablespoons lemon juice
- ¼ cup tablespoons vinegar
- 2 tablespoons soya sauce
- ½ teaspoon salt
- ½ teaspoon black pepper

Directions:

In large bowl add vinegar, brown sugar, lemon juice, chili flakes, garlic, soya sauce, black pepper and salt, Stir well.

17. Balsamic Rosemary Marinade

This simple marinade is an excellent choice for your pork.

Yields: 2 cups

Time: 8 mins.

Ingredients:

- 2 tablespoons dried rosemary
- 5 garlic cloves (chopped)
- 1-inch ginger slice (chopped)
- ½ cup olive oil
- ¼ cup balsamic vinegar
- ½ teaspoon salt

Directions:

In a zipped bag or bowl, add vinegar, olive oil, chopped ginger, pepper, chopped garlic, rosemary and salt. Mix well.

18. Brown Sugar and Maple Syrup Marinade

This marinade makes your pork an amazing meal for your guests.

Yields: 2 cups

Time: 15 mins.

Ingredients:

- 2 tablespoons rosemary (chopped)
- ¼ cup maple syrup
- 1 teaspoon garlic powder
- 3 tablespoons brown sugar
- 1 teaspoon thyme
- 2 tablespoons lemon juice
- ½ cup red wine vinegar
- 2 tablespoons olive oil
- ½ teaspoon salt
- ½ teaspoon black pepper

Directions:

In large bowl add brown sugar, maple syrup, olive oil, vinegar, lemon juice, garlic, vinegar, rosemary, thyme, salt, black pepper and mix to combine.

19. Mustard and Vinegar Marinade

This is the perfect marinade for your pork chops. It both tenderizes your meat and add flavor.

Yields: 1 cup

Time: 10 mins.

Ingredients:

- 4 tablespoon Dijon mustard
- ½ cup vinegar
- ½ teaspoon turmeric powder
- 1 teaspoon chilli powder
- 1 teaspoon garlic paste
- ½ teaspoon ginger paste
- 1 teaspoon salt

Directions:

In a bowl add Dijon mustard, vinegar, turmeric powder, chili powder, ginger paste, garlic paste, salt, and mix.

20. Spicy Fish Marinade

This marinade is fresh, spicy and fast. Can be made beforehand and refrigerate.

Yields: 1 ¼ cup

Time: 37 mins.

Ingredients:

- 6 tablespoons gram flour
- 1 teaspoon turmeric powder
- 1 teaspoon garlic paste
- 1 teaspoon cumin powder
- 1 teaspoon dry coriander powder
- 3 tablespoons lemon juice
- 3 tablespoons vinegar
- ½ teaspoon salt
- ½ teaspoon chili powder

Directions:

Add gram flour, turmeric powder, garlic paste, cumin powder, dry coriander powder, lemon juice, vinegar, salt, chili powder in a bowl and mix well.

21. Dijon Mustard and White Vinegar Fish Marinade

Use this tasty marinade to marinate your fish. The rich flavor will have your guest asking for more.

Yields: 1 cup

Time: 5 mins.

Ingredients:

- ½ cup white vinegar
- 3 tablespoons Dijon mustard
- 3-4 garlic cloves (chopped)
- 3 tablespoons lemon juice
- 1 teaspoon black pepper
- 1 teaspoon rosemary (chopped)
- ½ teaspoon cayenne pepper (chopped)

Directions:

In a bowl add vinegar, Dijon mustard, garlic cloves, lemon juice, salt, black pepper, rosemary, cayenne pepper and mix well.

22. Spicy Yogurt Beef Marinade

Marinating your beef in spicy yogurt gives it a great look and a bold taste.

Yields: 1 ¾ cup

Time: 15 mins.

Ingredients:

- 1 cup yogurt
- ½ teaspoon turmeric powder
- 1 teaspoon chili powder
- 1 teaspoon garlic paste
- ½ teaspoon ginger paste
- 1 teaspoon cumin powder
- ½ teaspoon cinnamon powder
- 3 tablespoons lemon juice

Directions:

In a bowl add yogurt, turmeric powder, chili powder, cinnamon powder, ginger paste, garlic paste, cumin powder, lemon juice, salt and mix well.

23. Hot Apple Cider Beef Marinade

This is a super quick marinade that adds some sweetness to your beef.

Yields: 2 ¼ cups

Time: 10 mins.

Ingredients:

- 1 cup apple cider vinegar
- 2 tablespoons chili flakes
- 1 teaspoon garlic paste
- 1 cup tomato ketchup
- 3 tablespoons lemon juice
- 1 teaspoon salt

Directions:

In a bowl add vinegar, chili flakes, tomato ketchup, garlic paste, lemon juice, salt and mix well.

24. Brandy Marinade

This marinade is fantastic on beef or pork tenderloin.

Yields: 1 cup

Time: 15 mins.

Ingredients:

- 1/2 cup port wine
- 1/2 cup brandy
- 1/2 tsp. dried tarragon
- 1/2 tsp. dried thyme
- 2 bay leaves
- 1 1/4 tsp. salt
- 1/2 tsp. black pepper
- 1/2 tsp. dry mustard

Directions:

Combine brandy, port wine, dried thyme, dried tarragon, salt, bay leaves, dry mustard and black pepper. Mix well.

25. Bourbon Marinade

Use this marinade on beef tenderloin, steaks or roast. Works perfect on almost anything.

Yields: 2 cups

Time: 15 mins.

Ingredients:

- 1 cup bourbon
- 1 cup water
- 2 tbs. lemon juice
- 2 tsp. Worcestershire sauce
- 1 tsp. Tabasco sauce
- 1 tsp. onion salt
- 1 tsp. lemon pepper seasoning
- 1 tsp. paprika

Directions:

Add to a mixing bowl, bourbon, lemon juice, water, Worcestershire sauce, tabasco sauce, lemon pepper seasoning, onion salt, paprika.

Stir until well combined.

26. Pepper Sage Marinade

Use this marinade on chicken or turkey.

Yields: 1 cup

Time: 10 mins.

Ingredients:

- 1/4 cup water
- 1/4 cup lemon juice
- 2 tbs. white wine vinegar
- 2 tbs. olive oil
- 2 tsp. Dijon mustard
- 1/4 cup chopped fresh sage
- 1 tsp. black pepper

Directions:

Add all the ingredients to a suitable sized mixing bowl. Stir until well combined.

27. Cranberry Marinade

This marinade is fabulous with chicken and turkey.

Yields: 1 ¾ cups

Time: 15 mins.

Ingredients:

- 1 cup cranberry juice cocktail
- 1/4 cup orange juice
- 1/4 cup olive oil
- 1 tsp. salt
- 1 tsp. black pepper
- 1/4 cup chopped fresh cilantro

Directions:

Add to a suitable sized mixing bowl all the ingredients. Stir until well combined. Pour the marinade over the poultry.

28. Honey Garlic Pork Marinade

This honey garlic Pork marinade makes the juiciest tender pork ever.

Yields: 2 cups

Time: 12 mins.

Ingredients:

- 3/4 cup lemon juice
- 3/4 cup honey
- 6 tbs. soy sauce
- 3 tbs. dry sherry
- 6 garlic cloves, (minced)

Directions:

Add all your ingredients, combining in a bowl then whisk well.

29. Garlic Basil Marinade

A perfect combination of flavors. Use the marinade on poultry or seafood.

Yields: 1 2/3 cups

Time: 15 mins.

Ingredients:

- 3/4 cup olive oil
- 1/2 cup tomato sauce
- 1 tsp. cayenne pepper
- 4 crushed garlic cloves
- 1/4 cup chopped fresh basil
- 1 tsp. salt
- 1/4 cup balsamic vinegar

Directions:

Add all your ingredients, combining in a bowl then whisk well. 3. Use to marinate your favorite fish or poultry dish.

30. Citrus Marinade

This citrusy marinade is perfect for poultry.

Yields: 2 cups

Time: 12 mins.

Ingredients:

- 1 cup orange juice
- 1/4 cup lime juice
- 1/4 cup olive oil
- 3 tbs. apple cider vinegar
- 2 tsp. salt
- 2 tsp. dried oregano
- 1 tsp. black pepper

Directions:

Add all your ingredients, combining in a bowl then whisk well. 2. Pour the marinade over the poultry.

Conclusion

And there you have it! 30 delicious marinade recipes to whip up in no time for the amateur home cook! Will you go with a classic and elegant recipe, or perhaps a messy but delicious is more to your liking? Whatever you choose, you'll end up with a delicious meal waiting to be devoured! I hope you had as much fun making these recipes as I've had coming up with them!

About the Author

A native of Indianapolis, Indiana, Valeria Ray found her passion for cooking while she was studying English Literature at Oakland City University. She decided to try a cooking course with her friends and the experience changed her forever. She enrolled at the Art Institute of Indiana which offered extensive courses in the culinary Arts. Once Ray dipped her toe in the cooking world, she never looked back.

When Valeria graduated, she worked in French restaurants in the Indianapolis area until she became the head chef at one of the 5-star establishments in the area. Valeria's attention to taste and visual detail caught the eye of a local business person who expressed an interest in publishing her recipes. Valeria began her secondary career authoring cookbooks and e-books which she tackled with as much talent and gusto as her first career. Her passion for food leaps off the page of her books which have colourful anecdotes and stunning pictures of dishes she has prepared herself.

Valeria Ray lives in Indianapolis with her husband of 15 years, Tom, her daughter, Isobel and their loveable Golden Retriever, Goldy. Valeria enjoys cooking special dishes in her large, comfortable kitchen where the family gets involved in preparing meals. This successful, dynamic chef is an inspiration to culinary students and novice cooks everywhere.

Author's Afterthoughts

Thank you for Purchasing my book and taking the time to read it from front to back. I am always grateful when a reader chooses my work and I hope you enjoyed it!

With the vast selection available online, I am touched that you chose to be purchasing my work and take valuable time out of your life to read it. My hope is that you feel you made the right decision.

I very much would like to know what you thought of the book. Please take the time to write an honest and informative review on Amazon.com. Your experience and opinions will be of great benefit to me and those readers looking to make an informed choice.

With much thanks,

Valeria Ray

Made in United States
Orlando, FL
15 September 2024